Pass the
CELERY,
ELLERY!

Illustrations by
Jeffrey Fisher
Text by
Gaga & Friends

Stewart, Tabori & Chang
New York

My thanks to Jeffrey, Leslie, Julie, Gretchen, Teresa, Xine, and Mitch and to my family of family and friends . . . for great art, bad rhymes, and a better book than I ever could have imagined. And most of all, to Gaga: this book belongs to you, and so do I. —CAH

Text and compilation copyright © 2000 Herter Studio
Illustrations copyright © 2000 Jeffrey Fisher

Concept and Creative Direction: Herter Studio,
432 Elizabeth Street, San Francisco, CA 94114 (email: books@herterstudio.com)
Art Direction and Design: Gretchen Scoble Design

Published in 2000 by
Stewart, Tabori & Chang
A division of U.S. Media Holdings, Inc.
115 West 18th Street
New York, NY 10011

Distributed in Canada by General Publishing Company Ltd.,
30 Lesmill Road, Don Mills, Ontario, Canada M3B 2T6

ISBN: 1-58479-031-8

Printed in Hong Kong

10 9 8 7 6 5 4 3 2 1
First Printing

to Sam, Frances, Pete,
& Samantha With love
from Gaga & Aunt Ki

for darlings Hero &
Georgia -JF

Around the table, one by one
Match food to name until You're done.

There are no rules except to rhyme
So pass the lime, sweet Clementine.

Pass the bread to Papa, Fred
Pass the ham to Sam instead.

Pass the carrOt, pass the corn!
Is Lena better than Bjorn?

Use all the letters – A to Z
Or just naMes that start with B.

Try Greek and Thai and Mexican
Go round the globe and back again.

Pass the Veggies, pass the cheese
Pass something Quickly would you please?!

Birthdays, breakfast, after lunch
Weekday suppers, Sunday brunch.

Anytime, anyWhere
Car rides, airplanes—we don't Care!

Six or sixty ways to play
This rhyme is dumb, so let's just say........

(please)

bread

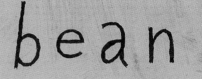

bean

son

Jerry

bun

berry

jean

fred

Chuck   duck

Fries

Fish

Food

Filet of sole

gum

chum

Pass the

Ham

Sam

Honey

Sonny

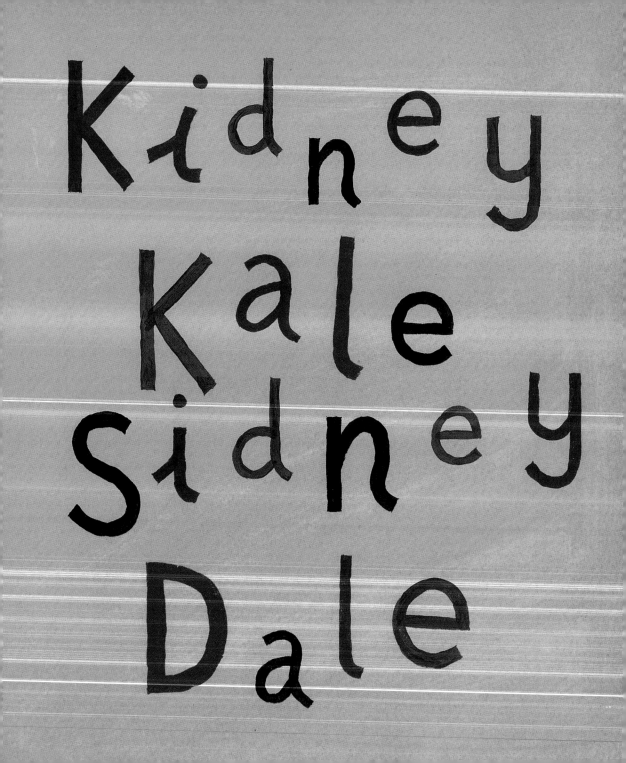

ZEEK TEENY

LEEK

LASAGNE

Pass the meat, Pete

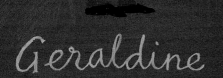

Geraldine

NUTMEG

Oleg

Nectarine

PASS THE

pasta

Jocasta

pan

pr

e

le

fran

pea

June

Vince

quince

Louis

ratatouille

Upside down cake

Jake

Emile  veal

xylophone!

Ted?

yam

Pass the zabaglione, Joni